SIX CHILDREN

MARK FORD

Six Children

faber and faber

First published in 2011
by Faber and Faber Ltd
Bloomsbury House
74–77 Great Russell Street
London WC1B 3DA

Typeset by Faber and Faber Ltd
Printed in England by T. J. International Ltd, Padstow, Cornwall

A CIP record for this book
is available from the British Library

ISBN 978–0–571–27332–4

821 FOR

2 4 6 8 10 9 7 5 3 1

In memory of my father

Acknowledgements

Acknowledgements are due to the editors of the following publications, in which some of these poems first appeared: *London Review of Books, The Nation, New York Review of Books, New Walk, Paris Review, PN Review, Poetry Review, Sienese Shredder, Times Literary Supplement.*

'John Hall' was first published in *Something Understood: Essays on Poetry and Poems for Helen Vendler.*

Contents

I

Dear and dear is their poisoned note,
The little snakes of silver throat,
In mossy skulls that nest and lie,
Ever singing 'die, oh! die.'

— THOMAS LOVELL BEDDOES

Dominion

Rise up! we heard their war cry – *Levitation!*
the trembling leaves kept sighing –
Levitation! Then Hurry Harry abandoned
the way of the raccoon and beaver, and felt
his heart whirled aloft by some hand
or talon: Oh no more, he reasoned, will I scramble
blindly between settlement and clearing, mocked
by the melancholy loon. Off – off – again
off, ye buckskin garments! How it glints,
my rifle, in the sun, as it arcs
towards the lake. And listen – on the stony beach
the ripples whisper, *Oh hurry*
Hurry Harry, oh Harry, hurry, hurry . . .

Invisible Hand

I

A white finger of frost along the spine
Of the country, and the first rumours of the first
Female Archbishop of Canterbury: while still
In her cradle the Lord filled
Her to the brim, and drove
Headlong the querulous demons whose riddles
End only in debt and pain; her dimpled
Right hand seemed to grasp and poise
A miniature crozier, and her eyes
Peered through tears at the sins of the world.

II

Weeping also, a woman in a coal-black dress says *Adios*
Amigo. She is fleeing
The grip of the huntsman, his suddenly
Drawn knife, his wispy moustache, harsh stubble
And secretly melting heart; through a tangle of russet
    briars
He watches her plunge into the woods
And be gone. Which way is home? The feathery bracken
Sighs and stirs, hisses around his knees, gets caught
In his gaiters. I spy, he thinks, with these tough stems
In my eye, something beginning with green.

III

He called me better looking than a newborn canary,
    then asked
If I was asking him to dance. A cheap shot,
I trilled back, from a cheapskate. But here, at any rate,
    was one

Sharp enough to descry the thread that ties
Cause and effect. In a wing beat we'd agreed on what
We'd need to learn to love: guilt,
Unending guilt . . . and after a few
Dizzying flutters of fear, that proved not so difficult. Let Rome
In Tiber melt, we'd cry, pirouetting
Through patient skies, high above the city's lights and sirens.

The Death of Petronius
after Tacitus

Turning to Caius Petronius, there are a few things about him
    that deserve
To be remembered: he liked to sleep all day, then devote his
    nights
To business – or pleasure. Most have to work hard
To become well-known, but it was idleness that propelled
Petronius to fame. He differed, though, from most debauchee
    or wastrel types,
For he was a cultured, exquisite master of the subtle arts
Of indulgence. His way of speaking, his way of doing things,
    seemed always casual,
Fresh and cool. Appointed governor of Bithynia, and then
    later consul, he also showed he could be an astute
And vigorous administrator.

                          At length, resuming his life of
vice – or apparent vice –
He found himself taken up by Nero, and admitted into the
    Emperor's coterie
Of intimates. They dubbed him 'Arbiter of Taste', and for a
    time Nero's sense
Of what was elegant or charming was determined wholly by
    Petronius. But this
So irked another of Nero's favourites, and voluptuaries,
    Tigellinus, that he hatched
A plot designed to appeal to the Emperor's overriding
    passion –
His cruelty. The Arbiter was framed
By a bribed slave, his household imprisoned, and his defence
Dismissed.

           Learning his fate

While at Cumae, Petronius at once abandoned
Both hope and fear – yet he refused simply to fling away
His life, either. Instead, having opened the veins
In his wrists, he'd let them bleed for a while; then, when the
    fancy
Moved him, have them bound up, then opened again, all the
    while
Chatting with friends about this and that, steering the
    conversation away
From serious topics that might make him seem brave
Or stoical. He lay back, listening to them recite
Not dreary reflections on the immortality of the soul or the
    nature
Of wisdom, but light songs and nonsense verse. Some of his
    servants
Received gifts, others a good flogging. Having dined
As usual, he slipped quietly into sleep – or was it death? –
As if it were the most natural thing in the world.

                                            While many
Doomed like Petronius compose deathbed testaments that
    shamelessly flatter
Whoever happens to be in power, his will contained a list
Of all the Emperor's most peculiar erotic tastes and extravagant
Sexual experiments, and the names of his partners
In crime, both men and women, willing and unwilling. He
    sent this
Under seal to Nero, then broke his signet ring: it, at least,
Would be innocent of the blood of others.

The Gaping Gulf

Cloud-capped, deserted, building and building site
Exchange whispers and winks. I glide half-
Asleep down the alley between them, as if
Adrift on some superannuated schooner. Nearby, on another
Kind of scaffold, John Stubbs gallantly raised his hat to the
    cheering crowd
With his left hand, and blessed the Queen, while her
Executioner held aloft his right.
                        Then he fainted. I've the taste
Of azure and wind in my mouth, and flecks
Of soot and dust in my hair. I think
Of all those on the verge of fainting
Today – teachers and alcoholics, long-distance runners,
    Tokyo-bound
Commuters crushed rib to rib. Their lungs
Wheeze and labour, and would rest; they need
A cold compress, a caressing breeze, some
Respite from the rattling drone of dried peas
In the inner ear. Ruminating, renouncing
Word after spellbound word, the alphabet looms like
    twenty-six
Patient camels on the horizon, then breaks
In half between the letters *m* and *n*, burdened
By too much grit
And rubble, and sand . . . Look! A sand-
Coloured lizard is disappearing through a hair-fine
Crack in the wall just above the wireless, as one gropes
For the dates of the reign of Henry
The Navigator, or Philip the Second
Of Spain. Dusk

[10]

Descends here like a thrown cloak, coarse, thick, almost
    suffocating,
Alive with inexplicable sounds. Was that
A distressed owl, or the harsh bark
Of a disease-bearing fox? What bothered who- or what-
Ever cried? – distant thunder vexing the dim
Hyades, or breadfruit upon breadfruit thudding
To earth?
          The gulf
Between a bleeding wrist and the breadfruit-crowned
Adventures of the current Order
Of the British Empire, is fast receding into the dark
Back of time. My father (born October, 1934, died
The last day of May, 2007) kept his medal in a safe
Cleverly hidden in the utility room.
The institutions that formed him, bade him don
A tin hat at Suez, shimmer like elegant, gauzy backdrops
Floating down from the flies. He wept
Rarely, ate powdered egg through gritted teeth
As a child, believed in the beneficent
Stride of progress. 'Who
Would true valour see,' we sang
At the crematorium, 'Let him
Come hither.'

Six Children

Though unmarried I have had six children
                   – WALT WHITMAN

The first woman I ever got with child wore calico
In Carolina. She was hoeing beans; as a languorous breeze
I caressed her loins, until her hoe lay abandoned in the furrow.

The second was braving the tumultuous seas that encircle
This fish-shaped isle; by the time a sudden riptide tore
Her from my grasp, she had known the full power of Paumanok.

One matron I waylaid – or was it *she* who waylaid
Me? – on a tram that shook and rattled and
Rang from Battery Park to Washington Heights and back.

O Pocahontas! You died as Rebecca Rolfe, and are buried
In Gravesend. Your distant descendant, her swollen belly
Taut as a drum, avoids my eye, and that of other menfolk.

While my glorious diva hurls her enraptured soul to the gods,
I sit, dove-like, brooding in the stalls; what in me is vast,
Dark and abysmal, her voice illumines and makes pregnant.

Some day, all together, we will stride the open road, wheeling
In an outsized pram my sixth, this broken, mustachioed
Soldier whose wounds I bind up nightly. His mother I forget.

International Bridge-Playing Woman

where must you wander? Macao, the Moluccas, a spa
near Minsk, as far as Montevideo? Do the hands
you lost haunt you? In aerodromes
and embassies the cards were shuffled, dealt,
assessed, while catch phrases whirred and chimed. Under
   a comic
pith helmet his supreme Loneliness, the ace
of trumps, divided the continents and time zones, braved
assegai and fever, emerged trembling from the interior
like pure prestige. The picture cards
leered roguishly as the Emperor's Band slid
into *'There's a long long trail a-winding, into*
the land of my dreams' . . . One
fled what one was, and the house where the towels had always
to be hung straight on the towel racks: – Since you must tear,
the quivering poplars whispered, yourself
bodily from your roots, let your thoughts
aerate and take wing; step
around the griffins, across the gravel, through
the dense, familiar shade cast by church
and church tower. May you
engage and defeat fear, strike even as home swells, blurs,
   or collapses
into a trick of air. While we
rustle and flex in the breeze, you will be floating
above squalor and sprawl, as remote and elusive
as a cloud. In the small hours,
in the lull before monsoon or typhoon
or insurrection or revolution, as the chambers of the heart
dilate, breathe in the night and let it stain

your blood, and obscure the lines
between black and red, chance and fate, abroad
and England. Either you belong
with those who belong, or you believe the stories
the cards tell, whether pieced together in windy
Mandalay, or in a small hotel *tout près de la place Pigalle*.

John Hall

Like Lord Cerimon he was familiar with the blest infusions
      That dwell in vegetives, metals, and stones:

He cured, he records, Michael Drayton of a tertian
      Fever with a spoonful of syrup of violets, and his own

Haemorrhoids with a pigeon he cut open alive, then
      Applied to his feet, to which it drew down

The vapours, while leeches set to work on his fundament.
      His beloved Susanna, Shakespeare's eldest, found

Relief from corruption of the gums and stinking breath, wind,
      Melancholy and cardiac passion in his potent ointment

Of roses, capon grease, sweet almonds and mallow water. Accounts
      Of his triumphs were kept in condensed Latin;

None of the cases published in *Select Observations*
      On English Bodies mentions his father-in-law's afflictions

Or demise. He himself died fighting a sudden and virulent
      Outbreak of the plague: 'Health is from the Lord.' (Amen.)

Lower Case

Using the heel
Of either hand, how I'd like to knock-
Knock-knock-knock some raw, devil-may-care
Spirit into the echoing chambers
Of the brain. Around
My cranium the churned-
Up air falls still, is hushed, save
Where the weak-eyed bat, with short
Shrill shriek
Flits by on leathern wing, tiny against the violet
Evening sky, or a scything blur
Across the twisted boughs and the white, waxy flowers
Of the frangipani trees.
                              Meanwhile, a blast
Of Shelltox
Dispatches another cockroach – it flips
Over twice, and its legs
Stop moving; its shiny brown shell, now beaded with
    poison, looks
Like a chain-smoker's nail. Through
A drifting mist of insecticide I hover
And roam, index finger
On the trigger, until the bitter fumes fade, and my interest
In killing what Shelltox kills
Fades . . . Relax
O muscles, in arms, neck, eyes and face – cast
Out remorse for this and other
Fits that wrench, wrench
And squeeze, squeeze and catch
In the throat. Let no man

Squirrel away what he owns, or thinks he owns, nor, ill
At ease in his own skin, swallow fire and so
Burn inwardly. As a fly
Eludes a motionless gecko's
Quicksilver tongue, and the whine of the generator
Dies away, I feel emptied, lighter
Somehow, as alert
As a blood-hungry mosquito; the heart's
Fibrillations are the earth
Turning, while my thoughts
Float free and under
The cool bristling grass, the damp stems
Disappearing into stringy roots, the tunnelled soil and
    gritty sand
And clay.
            Relax
O muscles, squirrel
Nothing away; let the churned-up air fall still,
Though a trigger finger hovers
In the violet night, a quicksilver, scything
Blur.

The Death of Hart Crane

Sir / Madam,

I was intrigued by the letter from a reader in your last issue
that recounted his meeting, in a bar in Greenwich Village in
the mid-sixties, a woman who claimed to have been a passen-
ger on the *Orizaba* on the voyage the boat made from Vera
Cruz to New York in April of 1932, a voyage that the poet
Hart Crane never completed. According to her Crane was
murdered and thrown overboard by sailors after a night of
such rough sex that they became afraid (surely wrongly) that
he might have them arrested when the boat docked in Man-
hattan. This reminded me of a night in the early seventies on
which I too happened to be drinking in a bar in Greenwich
Village. I got talking to an elderly man called Harold occupy-
ing an adjacent booth, and when the conversation touched
on poetry he explained, somewhat shyly, that he had himself
published two collections a long time ago, one called *White
Buildings* in 1926, and the other, *The Bridge*, in 1930. I asked
if he'd written much since. 'Oh plenty,' he replied, 'and a lot
of it much better than my early effusions.' I expressed an
interest in seeing this work, and he invited me back to his
apartment on MacDougal Street. Here the evening turns
somewhat hazy. I could hear the galloping strains of Ravel's
Boléro turned up loud as Harold fumbled for his keys. Clearly
some sort of party was in progress. At that moment the door
was opened from within by another man in his seventies,
who exclaimed happily, '*Hart*! – and friend! Come in!' The
room was full of men in their seventies, all, or so it seemed,
called either Hart or Harold. The apartment's walls were
covered with Aztec artefacts, and its floors with Mexican
carpets. It dawned on me then that Hart Crane had not only

somehow survived his supposed death by water, but that his vision of an America of the likeminded was being fulfilled that very night, as it was perhaps every night, in this apartment on MacDougal Street. At the same instant I realized that it was I, an absurd doubting Thomas brought face to face with a miracle, who deserved to be devoured by sharks.

Yours faithfully,

Name and address withheld

The Passing of the Passenger Pigeon

This bird used to be the most numerous on earth
And to blot out the sun for hours over Wisconsin and Michigan,
And to strip bare the great forests of cranberries, pine nuts and
acorns.

Whole trees toppled under the weight of roosting birds. In flight
They made a sound like Niagara Falls. Horses trembled,
And travellers made wild guesses at their numbers and meaning.

The bird's sad demise is chronicled on many websites. Children
Visit these for homework, and learn how far and fast the
passenger pigeon
Flew, and that its breast was red, and head and rump slate blue.

As the opulent sun set, raccoon-hatted hunters would gather
with pots
Of sulphur, and clubs and poles and ladders; in a trice they'd
transform the dung-
Heaped forest floor into a two-foot carpet of smouldering pigeon.

Being so common, they sold in the city for only a few pence
a dozen.
Farmers fed them to their pigs. By the century's end they had all
But joined the Great Auk and Labrador Duck in blissful oblivion.

The last known passenger pigeon was called Martha, after Martha
Washington. She died in Cincinnati Zoo on September 1st, 1914.
Her stuffed
Remains were transported to the capital, and there displayed in
the Smithsonian.

White Nights
after Lucretius

A snake, if a man's spittle
Falls upon it, will wriggle
And writhe in frenzied contortions, and may even gnaw
Itself to death; and there are certain
Trees, should you ever drift off to sleep
In their shade, you'd wake clutching your throbbing
  head as if an axe
Had been buried there. The blossom, I've heard, of a
  type of rowan
That flourishes in the mountains
Of Helicon has overpowered and killed with the vile stench
It emits. And women should be wary
Of the potent musk of the beaver, which can force a busy
  housewife
Suddenly to drop her darning, or her delicate needlework,
  and collapse
In a dead faint – though this
Occurs only if the scent is inhaled at the time when her
  menstrual
Blood is flowing.
                    Those afflicted with jaundice see everything
As yellow because their yellow bodies
Send out – like a halo or aura – a constant stream
Of tiny bright yellow seeds, and these seeds merge
With the images careering through the air from all that
  exists; and then a further
Coating of yellow is added by the patient's
Yellow eyeballs, which tinge all they absorb with their own
Lurid hue.

We humans did not, in my opinion,
Long ago slide from heaven
To here on some golden chain; nor did we emerge
From the ocean, nor were we created by the relentless
    pounding of waves
On rocks. It was the earth
Which bred us, as she feeds us still. Out of her own
Sweet will she created the wheat that shimmers, laden
Fruit trees, and buttercup meadows. But now nature
Seems tired; our farmers exhaust their oxen
And themselves, they blunt ploughshare
After ploughshare, but to little avail. The soil yields
    what it yields
Grudgingly, and demands more and more labour.
The wizened farmer sighs, and can't help
Thinking back to the days of his father, when things
Were simpler, and the fields more fertile, though far less
Of the world was cultivated. Likewise, the vineyard owner
Broods morosely on his twisted, stunted
Vines, and curses heaven, not realizing
That all things decay, that all things sink
Towards the grave, grow frail or weary, are worn gradually
Away by the remorseless passing
Of the years.

The Snare Unbroken

A nobler subject asks th' advent'rous song, sang
Mather Byles, then bade the Muse on soaring
Pinions rise. Goliah had to be defeated. In a secret

Haunt far removed from all the restless, glaring scenes
Of day, he communed alone, or with James Ralph
Observed the twinkling stars prepare their circuits. How

He envied Cotton Mather, who'd heard the war-whoop,
    and rejoiced
Over the rout of a band of roving Iroquois – *lo, their Mightiest
Are quelled, Salvage and Sagamore lie overturned, and fiery*

Foaming Blacks . . . their torsos, horridly streaked,
Their brawny flesh and prodigious bones, lay
Mouldering in some dappled forest clearing, picked clean

Eventually by crows. O citizens, let's catch
And pluck one, or more than one, and with every ink-
Black feather write of infernal regions of despair,

Of ghastly smiles and lidless eyeballs; of glittering
Temples and gay cities built on arid plains
And swamps, of silver mantling the moon sublime, and of

The snare that Satan set, unbroken.

Signs of the Times

'Today,' wrote Thomas Carlyle
As the brown and barge-laden Thames rolled past
Cheyne Walk, 'I am full of dyspepsia, but also
Of hope.' On the *Today*
Show today a dyspeptic interviewer set brusquely about
A hopeful minister, and I ingested, along with the dyspepsia
And the hope, a story about a dubious collector
Of Regency soft toys and Apache
Bows, arrow-flints, and tomahawks. Next
In line to be scalped was a corrupt
TV game-show host. Whither
The gentle, humane
Quizmastership of Magnus Magnusson, or the calm
   and bespectacled
Bamber Gascoigne?
                  Sweet day, so cool, so calm,
So bright, on which I don a shirt that cries out
For cufflinks, and sports
Embroidered initials on the right-hand cuff; on
Which I opened a desk drawer and discovered
A dozen or so pairs of sun-, half-rim- and reading-glasses
Beneath an essay in progress on the French
Revolution, and notes
Towards another on the Spanish Civil War. We
Were born in the forward-
Thinking sixties, and grew up in various capital cities
   in Africa
And Asia – wherever, that is, the British Overseas Airways
   Corporation
(BOAC, for short) saw fit. In Lagos

The gardener earned a trifling bonus for each
Black mamba he destroyed
With his machete; they lurked mainly in the cool
Of the garage, curled behind the whitewall
Tyres of our sturdy Zephyr, deaf to the shouting and rifle-
    fire
Of the barracks adjacent, and military sirens tearing
Open the heavy heat.
                        It took – or seemed
To take – no time at all for the venom to prove, point
By careful point, what it meant. I found
Myself sweating too, trying
To recall the serpentine journeys made by adventurers
    such as Mungo Park
And Richard Burton, and the weeping jungles
And empty deserts they traversed. Unsheathed, their
    bone-
Handled bush knives whispered
Like settling locusts or long-
Promised waterfalls. One sticky morning
John Hanning Speke awoke on a spur above Lake
Tanganyika with a ferocious headache,
Blind as an earthworm. The clear lake waters rippled
And sighed, then flared like a peacock's tail beneath
    the whitening sky.

They Drove

just terribly, but humorously sang
Jonathan Richman's 'Stop This Car' after each sudden

swerve or rubbery squeal. Once they discussed
the pros and cons of having sex

with Bob Dylan – or a Bob Dylan look-alike – in a Buick
while listening to 'From a Buick 6'.

Black fumes billowed from the exhaust, and by a species
of dead reckoning they charted, in a road atlas, detours

and punctures, losses and gains – all
the time wondering whether (as Van Morrison once

sang) to 'Hardnose
the Highway' were the same as to live.

Hourglass

Early August, and the chestnuts
Are wilting – their splay leaves
Tattered and blotched, their shadows, not understood,
    speaking
A forgotten tongue . . . tell, tell us where, their drugged
    sap
Must be sighing, tell us where our distress
Ends, where
Are the victories? Each pinched, each
Aching hour we grow sadder
And stranger: a rift
In the billowing cloud cover, this cage
Of rain, soft greyish
Swarms of nameless insects circling, alighting,
Settling, sustaining themselves,
A sandy, pockmarked
Wormcast, the deft sideways hop
And jab of a predatory
Speckled starling – are the shreds and fraying
Filaments
An irresolute wind
Is teasing
Apart, winnowing
And dispersing, strand
By strand by strand.

*

'See,' I grieved, 'his mind
That so filtered
And sifted nature it made transparent her weirdest secrets,
    now lies
A broken prisoner of night. His neck
Droops, as if bowed with chains, and he sees nothing
But the cold, gaping ground.' At this, fixing me
With her gimlet eyes, the strange woman answered:
    'But surely you
Are one of those who once lapped at my breast, and
    were raised
To tough-minded
Maturity on what I fed you? I armed you as well, yet
    you threw away
My weapons, not realizing
They would have kept you safe. Now
Do you recognize me? . . . You don't speak. Is it shame
Or stupefaction that keeps you silent? How I wish
It were shame!' Then, when she saw
My tongue and lips had utterly frozen, she approached
And laid a soothing hand
On my torso: 'We must wait,' she murmured, 'for this fit
To pass. He'll know me soon enough, and then
Himself. For the moment let me wipe
Away some of the worries obscuring, like thick
    storm clouds,
His troubled sight.' So speaking, she folded her dress
Into a pleat, and reached out, and with it dried my
    streaming eyes.

*

Through
The valley ran a brook
In full spate. I descended, and passed a middle-aged
    woman kneeling
At its edge. She was washing potatoes. When I travel,
    I travel
Light, with just a few things in a knapsack, no sword
Hangs from my belt. And with my shaven head
I look like a priest, but I'm not, for I'm powdered
All over, from crown to foot, with the dust
Of the world . . . I reached home
Just as the leaves
Were turning, and my brothers and sisters
Gathered round, excitedly; but all I saw were wrinkles,
    dewlaps,
White eyebrows, and watery eyes. My older brother
Pressed into my hand a small purse, and said,
'Open it.' Inside were a few strands of white hair
Preserved in a tiny glass case as relics
Of our mother. Nothing was the same, and it seemed
A miracle we were ourselves
Still alive. While I balanced
The frail, intertwined hairs in the palm
Of my hand, I kept imagining my tears
Dissolving them, their melting as an early autumn frost
Melts in morning rain.

II

Open the book. (The gilt rubs off the edges of the pages and pollinates the fingertips.) Open the heavy book.

— ELIZABETH BISHOP

After Africa

After Africa, Surbiton:
An unheated house, and flagstone pavements;
No colobus monkeys, no cheetahs scouring the plains.
Verrucas and weeping blisters ravaged our feet.

An unheated house, and flagstone pavements,
And snow falling through the halos of street lamps;
Verrucas and weeping blisters ravaged our feet;
But the shavings made by our carpenter, Chippy, were
    as soft as bougainvillea flowers

Or snow falling through the halos of street lamps.
Everyone was pale, pale or grey, as pale or grey
As the shavings made by our carpenter, Chippy, which
    were soft as bougainvillea flowers . . .
Red, African dust spilled from the wheels of our toy
    trucks and cars.

Everyone was pale, pale or grey, as pale or grey
As the faded carpet on which
Red, African dust spilled from the wheels of our toy
    trucks and cars.
Real traffic roared outside.

A faded carpet on which
Everything seemed after Africa; Surbiton's
Real traffic roared outside –
No colobus monkeys, no cheetahs scouring the plains.

Ravished

Is the night
Chilly and dark? The night is chilly
But not dark. An all but full
April moon
Slides above barely visible clouds, and is greeted
By a burst of hooting from an urban
Tawny owl. On empty
Brownfield sites they nest, and rear their young, and feed
On vermin. Has
Any
Probing, saucer-eyed astronomer, even a modern
Or French one, ever
Grown genuinely accustomed '*aux profondeurs du grand
Vide céleste*'? Someone halts, and broods
In the deserted doorway of a Chinese
Emporium, someone
Is struggling to rise swiftly
From his chair.

*

A pair of empty
Curly brackets might have been
His colophon, I thought, parting one night
At closing time
On Great Russell Street, outside our last port of call,
    the Museum
Tavern. Between his thick-
Soled hiking boots rested a battered duffel bag with a
    single yellow

Shin pad protruding. A group
Of youthful party-goers sashayed by – one wearing a
    traffic cone
On her head: '*like*
*A complete unkn_ooown_*,' a voice from the pack
Intoned . . . I was picturing the shiny black
Cab he so imperiously
Hailed whisking him west, revving, cruising, braking, gliding
Across junctions, the driver
At length twisting around, awaiting payment, as I veered
And tacked through the eerily silent
Squares of Bloomsbury, towards Euston.

Gregory of Nazianzus

stretched out on the grass, and tried
to relax. A delightful breeze stirred his beard
but his ear canals ached, and his tongue
felt bloated. While there is blood
in these veins, he mused, and I can hear
the murmur of leaves, and sparrows sing, I will not despair.

He half-dozed, and in a waking dream relived the despair
that had seized him during a stormy voyage from Alexandria
   to Athens. Death had tried
and tested him then. He'd shouted a prayer, but all he
   could hear
were the howling winds and surging seas, and the sailors
   cursing: 'Your white-bearded
God seems a trifle deaf,' one taunted; the blood
drained from his face, but he refused to hold his tongue.

'And once in Athens,' he reflected, startled awake by a falling
   pinecone, 'how my tongue
loosened, and poured forth God's word; even Basil despaired
of rivalling my eloquence . . . Basil . . . in Athens we lived
   together like blood-
brothers, sharing cramped lodgings, frugal meals, our
   innermost thoughts . . . I tried
so often, to write to you . . . I see you now, your hair oiled,
   your beard
neatly trimmed, leaning into me, as if my words were all you
   ever wished to hear . . .

'Who lured me to Constantinople? that city of angels – and do
    The people flocked to hear
the Holy Spirit move my lips, but many were swayed by the lies of
    that silver-tongued
viper, Maximus the Cynic, his glossy beard
all drenched with spittle and crocodile tears, his clothes rent in
    despair
at the hell fires being stoked for my followers. Brazen calumnies . . .
    yet when I tried
to refute them, the crowd hooted and hissed me, and hurled stones,
    drawing blood.'

As the rays of the sinking sun slanted through cypress and pine,
    Gregory's blood
cooled. He thought he could hear
his houseboy shouting his name, and he tried
to respond, but couldn't, for his tongue
seemed glued to his palate. He felt the slow encroachment of despair.
Something was crawling through his beard.

Gloomily he resumed his train of thought: 'My poor beard
was not only matted, but stained a deep crimson with my
    own blood
as I cried to the Lord, not in despair,
but joyfully, believing He would hear
and gather me up, and that cherubim and seraphim would soon,
    and with one tongue,
be exalting me . . . now I fear I was tried,

tried and found wanting . . .' Stroking his beard,
he observed the flickering tongue of a lizard, and waited for
    the blood
to return to his own. He could hear his houseboy's cries receding,
    and in his voice a note of despair.

[39]

A Natural History

                    . . . the river's
ıᴄᴇ closes; silvery carp, whiskered and scaly
As dragons, cluster
And thrash around the piers
Of the bridge. Frogs,
Eels, water rodents
Die. On the bank, preserved like impurities
In glass, a rutty tangle of wheel tracks, of paw-
And hoof-prints, of sandal- and boot-prints. At intervals
I found fire-
Ravaged altars, some blackened, some
Still smouldering; pools
Of congealed blood, from either an offering or perhaps
A wound, lay in the hollows
Of the uneven floors. Near one
I knelt and fingered
The shards of a pot, or water clock, painted bright red
And pink, like a fuchsia; tucked
Up under the eaves of another, an abandoned
Bird's nest, fabricated in a curious manner
From scraps of wool, and brown animal hair, and a few
     fragments, torn but still
Just legible, of papyrus . . .

                    . . . now the Magi
Who are all
Appalling liars, believe the gods will never appear to, nor
     obey,
A person with freckles. To one who has a fishbone
Lodged in the throat, they say, 'Plunge

[40]

Your feet in freezing water'; but if it's a crust
That's stuck there, the remedy is bread from the same loaf
Rammed into both ears. Headaches
Are best cured, they claim, by pouring vinegar
Over door-hinges, and applying the resultant sludge
To the temples. They venerate the mole, and trust
The entrails of no creature as they trust
Those of this tiny blind tunneller through the bowels
Of the earth. Anyone who consumes a mole's heart, fresh
And still beating, will see like a prophet
Into the future. Avoid
Using a vulture's feather as a tooth pick; for sweet breath
Rub the ashes of burnt mice mixed with honey
Around the gums, then clean
With a porcupine quill. Should you suffer
From persistent pain in the abdomen, tear open
A bat . . .

     . . . beyond
Stretches a desert where flickering ghosts crowd
Round the startled traveller, then vanish. Nature
Would have us wonder
At her ingenuity, and creates men who never spit,
Who stand all day watching the burning sun journey across
    the sky, moving
Only to shift their weight from foot
To foot. Some are born with two pupils
In one eye, and in the other, if you look
Closely, you will see the image of a horse. There are regions
Where no shadows
Ever fall, where men sleep but do not dream, where human
Skulls serve as water vessels. Those on whose mouths
A swarm of bees settled when they were young, will sway

Whole peoples with their clear
Golden words in later life. But no
Words spoken of any kind, in any tongue, can allay
The griefs of ageing, or deny our racked bodies their final,
    sweet
Release into oblivion: sure signs
Of impending death include numbness, raucous laughter,
    mottled
Eyes or nostrils, fingers toying obsessively with the
    tasselled
Fringe of the bedspread . . .

The Münster Anabaptists

I

The scribes
of Strasbourg gazed in wonder
at the soaring tower; inside was a cage
in which the itinerant preacher
Melchior Hoffman
was imprisoned, his wanderings
over; 'Woe,' wailed
Melchior Hoffman, night and day, hour
after hour, rattling the iron bars
of his cage, 'Woe
will engulf you, *you*, O damned
and sinning scribes of Strasbourg.'

II

We saw it – a cloud in the shape of an angry bishop
Looming over us, dwarfing us; and we gasped as a blade
Of lightning tore apart the cloud, and it dissolved as the
   sun set.

So we drove the unclean from Münster, laughing
As they fled, unbaptised and naked, into knifing winds
And frenzied snow; and Jan Matthys, our bony prophet,
   was content.

And he decreed all money, and all silver and gold, be
   surrendered, and all
Legal deeds, and books, save the Bible, be burned; for the
   Kingdom
Of God was at hand, and doubters, like this querulous
   blacksmith, must die.

And some sang a hymn, and praised gaunt, fiery Jan
    Matthys, the Lord's
Anointed, once a baker in Haarlem, while some crawled
On their knees across the marketplace, imploring forgiveness.

And daily the hirelings besieging us were touched by the
    Lord, and laid down
Their arms, and were admitted to Münster; and in Münster
    they heard
Jan Matthys declare the siege, and the world, would end
    this Easter.

Encased in armour, lo! our own Gideon rides forth through
    the city gates
Leading his tiny band of chosen followers; and we, from the
    walls of Münster, watch
The bishop's *landsknechts* quail, and brace themselves
    for slaughter.

Dithering

'Let Spades be trumps!' she said, and trumps they were; it leaves
us free to cry, and whisper to their souls to
go. Nor wilt thou
then forget where are the legs with which
you run, Hurroo! Hurroo!, or wake
and feel the fell of dark. Like an angel came
I down,
when my dream was near the moon,
the crux left of the watershed, and the stars that usher
evening rose. He
is not here; but far away – o'er Bodley's dome his future labours
spread. 'Have you been
out?' 'No.' 'And don't want to, perhaps?' Men shut their doors
against a setting sun, and high
the mountain-tops, in cloudy air, and instantly the whole
sky burned with fury against them. They
like to drink beer, and each one had
a little wicker basket, made of fine twigs, entrailed curiously:
patient, look, thou watchest the last oozings hours by hours,
etherized
upon a midnight dreary, where no flower can wither; many
a spring I shoot up fair, the book on the writing
table, the hand in the breast pocket.

Rinse and Repeat

The Zabbaleen left drought-stricken rural Egypt for Cairo in
the 1950s.
Our unique formula helps condition and smooth damaged
hair.

They brought their pigs, which they fed with the city's
discarded scraps and peelings.
Drench with water, then massage deeply into scalp and roots.

Soon the Zabbaleen had evolved into a vast, informal
garbage team.
There's more to life than hair, but it's a good place to start.

Young Zabbaleen scavengers attend a school called 'Spirit
of Youth'.
Rich in essential oils – take a deep breath and enjoy the
delicious smell.

'Spirit of Youth' is sponsored by a manufacturer of bottles
of shampoo.
Boost and volumise lifeless hair by removing dirt and debris
that weigh hair down.

Sorting and studying empty bottles of shampoo, young
Zabbaleen learn to read and write.
Avoid contact with eyes – should this occur rinse immediately
with clean, warm water.

Decree Nisi

On this crescent beach, sorrow; tell me
About it, digger
Of cockles and clams.

*

Wearing new aviator
Ray-Bans at night, I see myself
In grainy miniature: trigger-happy, falling.

*

The last weekend in May; Broadstairs'
Moonlit arcades, and cormorants'
Cries stretched across the water.

*

As the octopus dreams
In the octopus pot, I gather leaves and grass
And feathers to throw at shadows, silhouettes.

Masse und Macht

One Inch
of Emotion, One Inch
of Ash, I read, in fiery letters, on a skin-
tight T-shirt
passing, a little too close, at rush-hour, under the
　　soaring stanchions
of Hungerford Bridge. Some
reflex that verged
on a shiver
set me thinking of Elias
Canetti, and how he claimed that we hate
to be touched, however
gently, in a slow-moving crowd, and so
apologise profusely when we brush
against a stranger. Looming

looming up through
the haze, Charing Cross, its maw
agape, its tentacles twitching
and probing. A busker, cross-
legged, hunched beneath the balustrade, was merrily
　　tooting 'The Bard
of Armagh' into a child's
pink, see-through recorder – occasionally
plucking it from his lips
so he could sing
in a reedy voice: 'And when Sergeant Death
in his cold arms shall embrace me, oh lull me to sleep
with sweet Erin Go Bragh . . .' Beyond
and beneath swirled
the Thames, at once

murky and aflame. I watched,
blinking, the setting sun
catch and burnish the glass and flanks of the cabs
and buses, the opaque 4x4s
and low-roofed cars and sleek
tourist coaches
crawling across Waterloo Bridge; an almost
empty inbound commuter train clanked slowly
by . . . In the lull that ensued, the merry busker's
    tooting grew
hauntingly erratic, then died
away, and with a dip
of the shoulder I surged on, through a swarm of
    chattering
language students, all carrying light-blue knapsacks,
    and filling
the air with the strains of their dear

native land.

Wooster and Jeeves

*. . . it was to the English colonist like a revolt of the domestic
staff . . . It was as though Jeeves had taken to the jungle*
      – GRAHAM GREENE, *Ways of Escape*

Malaria, sleeping sickness, bilharzia, yellow fever – Wooster
had seen them all afflict his faithful Jeeves;
now a new disease was rife among the Kikuyu,
carried not by mosquitoes or tsetse flies, but on the tip of a *simi*
     or *panga*.
The shrieking of baboons seemed deafening as he stepped
onto the veranda, and scanned the horizon, muttering a mild oath.

Even his own docile houseboy had succumbed, he suspected, and
     taken the vile oath,
had lapped up a gourd of goat's blood (Bertie Wooster
shuddered at the thought) then stuck a thorn seven times into the
     goat's eyeball. Under the steps
to an outhouse he'd found bloodstained banana leaves. Summoned,
     Jeeves
just shook his head, and murmured, '*Mau Mau . . . panga . . .*
Bwana beware . . .' Beneath, coiled like a snake, was an animal
     intestine the Kikuyu

believed had magical powers . . . closing his eyes, Bertie recalled
     the first Kikuyu
he'd hired, and the private oath
to treat them kindly that he'd made; their *pangas*
caught the sun, and flamed when they moved. The rich red soil
     of Wooster
Farm was perfect for sisal and maize; he set to work some fifty Jeeves
to clear the bush, and plough the land, and together, step by step

they battled the wilderness . . . Abruptly, dusk fell. Shrouded
    figures were stepping
out of the Aberdare forest, heading for an isolated homestead
    or Kikuyu
collaborator. Their leader, Colonel Jeeves,
whistled like a bird, and his men advanced. Tonight an oath-
breaking traitor, or maybe a Wooster
would wake to an unfamiliar noise, and moonlight on a falling
    panga.

'Is this,' the British Club's leading man demanded, clutching
    the air, 'a *panga*
which I see before me, the handle toward my hand?' Steps
on the gravel prated softly of watchmen guarding young
    Woosters –
that, or the approach of murder most foul. The Kikuyu
rebel must be unseamed from the nave to the chops, the hateful
    oath
retracted, and poor deluded Jeeves

restored to his senses. It was decreed, therefore, that any Jeeves
or witchdoctor caught killing a sheep or a goat with a *panga*
in order to administer a Mau Mau oath
of allegiance, must die. The guilty mounted the steps
to makeshift gallows, commending their souls to their Kikuyu
Ngai. The last thing they saw was the razor wire of Camp
    Wooster.

One morning Bertie Wooster was studying the newspaper.
    Many Jeeves
had come and gone. But was this dead Kikuyu, his *panga*
by his side, the one who'd stopped him stepping on a cobra? Yes,
    it *was* him, he'd take an oath!

Released

to wander
between the winds, and find
no home, to scour
the thickets for hips, frail
wisps
of animal fur or fluff, picnic
detritus, water
as it trickles between rustling
ferns or oozing, densely
wadded layers
of leaves . . .

ka-
boom ka-boom, the heart
pounds, while
blood as red as holly berries
stains the shepherd's purse on which
he wakes. The far-
off murmur
of waves breaking
on shingle throbs
and burns in his fevered
eardrums; following
his own
scarlet trail through campion and saxifrage
    and sweet
cicely, he stumbles
downhill, from trampled
copse to ravaged clearing, a cloud
of flies

about his groin. Curious
gulls wheel, shrieking, around the lip
of the cliff
he finally reaches, above an empty, iron-
grey sea.

'My mind,'
he wails, 'has grown
keen as the razor-
edged steel I pressed
against, and then into, and through my soft, secret
flesh . . . oh years, how was it
you led to this? I, the acknowledged
flower of the gymnasium, my lintels decked
each sunrise with orchids, am now
self-plucked, doomed to prowl
these barren, savage tracts, forever, and serve . . .'

The dread
Cybele has heard
enough: unleashing
the left-hand lion
from her chariot's traces, she lowers
her pale mouth
to his pricked and tawny ear, and whispers, 'Go,
ferocious one, go, and scare
this lily-
livered acolyte, so that never
again will he dream of straying
from the groves and streams sacred
to my law. Lash
yourself forward with your swingeing tail, until I
    can feel

the land tremble
under your thundering paws.' The yoke
pin lifted, he bounds
in a rabid frenzy towards the hapless,
grieving Attis. As the lion
springs, Attis screams
to Cybele, begs
Cybele, his tormentor, his goddess, for help.

Bist du ein König?

The landlord of the Inn of the Two Herrings
watched, yawning, the afternoon rain
pockmark the dust, and dimple the grey-green

harbour waters: out on the washing line, his sodden
breeches would be staying
sodden. No need to water the flowerpots. A fitful wind

wailed in the chimney breast, now
and then loosening
a clump of soot that came pattering down

into the hearth. He plucked with his nails
at his collar, but couldn't reach
the itch. His wife, the first of seventeen, was upstairs

with the babies, who, like
the wind, were wailing; and over their wailing he
    could hear
her yelling at him to find

and bring the gripe water . . . the collar
was not just
itchy, but metal, and spiked, and when he protested,
    the fire tongs

leapt from beside the hearth, a deep
fiery orange. Alarmed, he called out
for a wife to hand him the poker, so he could fend

[55]

off the tongs, but in his distress named
the shrewish one, Elizabeth,
whom in a fit of pique, he'd himself

beheaded. The tongs
advanced, with glowing, open jaws, while the wind
sang a hymn; its chorus

seemed to consist of two
questions asked over and over: *Where
is the gripe water? Bist*

du ein König?

Decree Absolute

                           . . . pink-
veined blossoms falling, the face, lightly
tattooed, of a god
carved, frowning,
into the bole
of a lime-tree . . . *tchack-tchack tsk*
tchack-tchack
tsk laments
a fidgety stonechat, inflating
his rusty breast, his wings and tail
a blur; one
restless, beady eye
fastens on a tiny, green-shelled snail gliding
over a shadowy patch of roots
and drifted petals
and moss.

The Confidence Man

I dreamt some children I'd never met were playing at
being Hölderlin walking to Bordeaux. One carried a
bulging canvas knapsack on his back, and was wear-
ing knee-breeches, a collarless jacket, a three-cornered
hat, and a pair of stout leather boots; his clothes were
powdered white with the dust of the road. Another
periodically shook his fist at the flawless skies, and
cried out 'Susette! Susette! oh my Susette!' whenever
he stumbled, or paused to rest. The third, a flaxen-
haired girl, floated some distance in front; dressed in
gingham, she advanced swiftly, but seemed to move
neither her legs nor her arms, which dangled limply
at her sides; over her head hung a searing white halo.

*

I sat
in the dark ivy, listening. These
fibrous networks
of arteries
and nerves are to alter
the way air itself enters
and leaves
the lungs. Through me
the voices of plover, of the ousel, of curlew, of buzzard
and snipe; and with this
fingernail
I flicked a pair of glittering ladybirds
as they mated on the curled leaf
of an apple tree, in May.

Fragments

When dawn, wearing golden sandals, awoke me,
I began to crawl, burning, shivering, to my uncurtained
    window;
Migrating birds streamed over the dark sea.

Who can quench the ingenious fires of cruelty?
I was dreaming of white-fetlocked horses conferring in
    a meadow
When dawn, wearing golden sandals, awoke me.

On my stopped loom, a sort of landscape: icy
Peaks, serrated as daggers; a corpse, and beside it a crow,
And migrating birds streaming over the dark sea.

Fat, autumnal flies alight on my sheets, rainbow-hued,
    dizzy;
This one on my wrist – its mandibles quiver, its gibbous
    eyes glow . . .
Then dawn, wearing golden sandals, awoke me.

Merciless daughter of Zeus, immortal Aphrodite,
Come to me, sing to me, low-voiced, in sorrow
Of migrating birds that stream over the dark sea.

Cast aside your spangled headband; in my mirror I see
You beneath these stringy locks, puckered lips and
    tearstained cheeks . . . go,
Migrating birds, stream over the dark sea;
And dawn, wearing golden sandals, awake me.

Notes

'The Death of Petronius' is adapted from a passage in Book 16 of *Annales* by Tacitus.

'White Nights' is adapted from various passages in *De Rerum Natura* by Lucretius.

The second part of 'Hourglass' is adapted from a section of *De Consolatione Philosophiae* by Boethius, the third, from a work by Matsuo Bashō called *Nozarashi kikō*, a title variously translated as *Journal of Bleached Bones in a Field*, *Travelogue of Weather-Beaten Bones* and *The Records of a Weather-Exposed Skeleton*.

'Ravished' is an elegy for the poet Mick Imlah (1956–2009).

Parts of 'A Natural History' are adapted from various passages of *Naturalis Historia* by Pliny the Elder.

'Dithering' is a cento inspired by the opening lines of T. S. Eliot's 'The Love Song of J. Alfred Prufrock'.

'Released' is based on the story of Attis in Catullus LXIII.

'*Bist du ein König?*' ('Are *you* a king?'): this was the question scornfully put to Jan van Leyden by Bishop Franz von Waldeck on the Bishop's triumphant entry into Münster, after a seventeen-month siege. ('*Und bist du ein Bischof?*' Jan is said to have replied.) King Jan and two other leaders of the Anabaptist rebellion, Bernard Knipperdolling and Bernard Krechting, were executed on 22 January 1536; each was first tortured for an hour with red-hot tongs, then stabbed in the heart with a dagger. The name of the wife Jan van Leyden beheaded was Elizabeth Wandscheer.

'Fragments' makes use of a number of images from the poetry of Sappho.